FAVORITE CATHO

Written by Carol Ann Morrow

Illustrated by Miguel D. Lopez

ISBN 1-936020-12-6

Artwork and Text © 2011 Aquinas Kids, Phoenix, Arizona.

Saints Michael, Gabriel, and Raphael are archangels. They are messengers and protectors of God's people. You can also be messengers of good news.

Saints Joachim and Anna were the parents of Mary and the grandparents of Jesus. Jesus loved His grandparents. If you have grandparents, be sure to tell them you love them.

Saint Joseph was the foster father of Jesus. He took good care of Mary and her Son. You can also ask Saint Joseph to protect and watch over you.

Saint John the Baptist was the cousin of Jesus. He led many people to follow Jesus. You can also lead people to follow Jesus by your example.

Saint Peter was a fisherman. Jesus chose Peter to be the leader of all His followers. He asked Peter three times, "Do you love me?" What would you say to Jesus?

Saint Mary Magdalene was the first person at the tomb to see Jesus when He rose from the dead. She told the disciples, "I have seen the Lord!" Where have you seen Jesus today?

Saint Stephen was stoned to death because he believed in Jesus. He prayed for the people who were hurting him.

Saints Mathew, Mark, Luke, and John wrote the four Gospels.
The Gospels teach us about Jesus and help us to follow Him.
Color these symbols of the Gospel writers.

Matthew

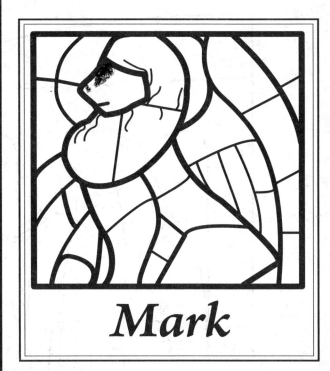

Mark

Luke

John

Saint Timothy was a young helper of the great apostle Saint Paul. Paul said to him, "Let no one look down on you for your youth." Young as you are, you can also help other people to know Jesus.

Saint Valentine was imprisoned when he cured the blindness of his jailer's daughter. He then left her a note—the very first valentine. Today, we send valentines to show our friendship and love.

Saint Blaise helped a child cough up a fishbone that was choking him. We ask Saint Blaise to protect us from diseases of the throat.

Saint Monica was the mother of Saint Augustine. She worked and prayed very hard to help her husband, her mother-in-law, and her son become believers in Jesus. Your prayers are powerful too.

Saint Nicholas was a bishop who helped poor young women by secretly giving them bags of gold. They used the money for their marriage. Today's Santa Claus was inspired by Saint Nicholas.

Saint Patrick taught the people of Ireland about the Holy Trinity by showing them a shamrock. A shamrock has three leaves on one stem. Shamrocks and three-leaf clovers are a favorite of Irish people today.

Saint Isidore was a married farmer who gave some of his crops to the poor and cared well for his animals. Do you take care of your plants and pets?

Saint Francis of Assisi thought his work was to repair churches that were falling down. Later, he saw that he was to help the Church and its people to be strong. Can you help someone be strong in their love for Jesus?

Saint Anthony of Padua spoke tenderly and fervently of Jesus.
The crowds who came to hear him were not able to fit in the
churches. Saint Anthony spoke outdoors while people picnicked
and listened. How well do you listen in church?

Our Lady arranged roses within the cloak, or tilma, of Saint Juan Diego to convince the bishop that she had appeared to him. When Juan Diego opened his tilma, the bishop saw the image of Our Lady of Guadalupe! Take a message of love to someone today.

Saint Martin de Porres was the child of a black woman whose father would not claim him. He could have been angry, but instead he helped the poor and hungry in Peru. Thank your parents for their care.

Saint Margaret Mary Alacoque encouraged people to love the Sacred Heart of Jesus. Do you keep a love for Jesus in your heart—as He keeps you in His?

Blessed Kateri Tekakwitha was a Native American whose people lived in New York. She liked to make little crosses and leave them along her path to remind her of Jesus. Do you have a crucifix in your room?

Saint John Bosco was a priest and a teacher of young people. He helped many poor boys who had no parents. Say thank you to the people who teach you.

Pope Pius X changed the rules to allow children to receive Holy Communion when they were 7 or 8. Aren't you glad? When you receive Holy Communion, tell Jesus you love Him.

Saint Damien of Molokai chose to serve on an island where people with leprosy were sent away to die. He made them happier and more comfortable. Then he got the disease himself. You can help someone who needs you.

Saint Therese of Lisieux died when she was only 24 years old. She became a saint by doing little things—like washing the dishes—out of love for Jesus. Can you help wash the dishes with love today?

Saint Maximilian Kolbe was a Franciscan priest put in prison by the Nazis. He volunteered to take the place of a young father who was going to be killed. How can you be brave for Jesus?

Blessed Mother Teresa of Calcutta accepted the call of Jesus to serve the poorest of the poor. She worked for forty years among the poor, elderly, and sick people of India. Help someone who is older today.

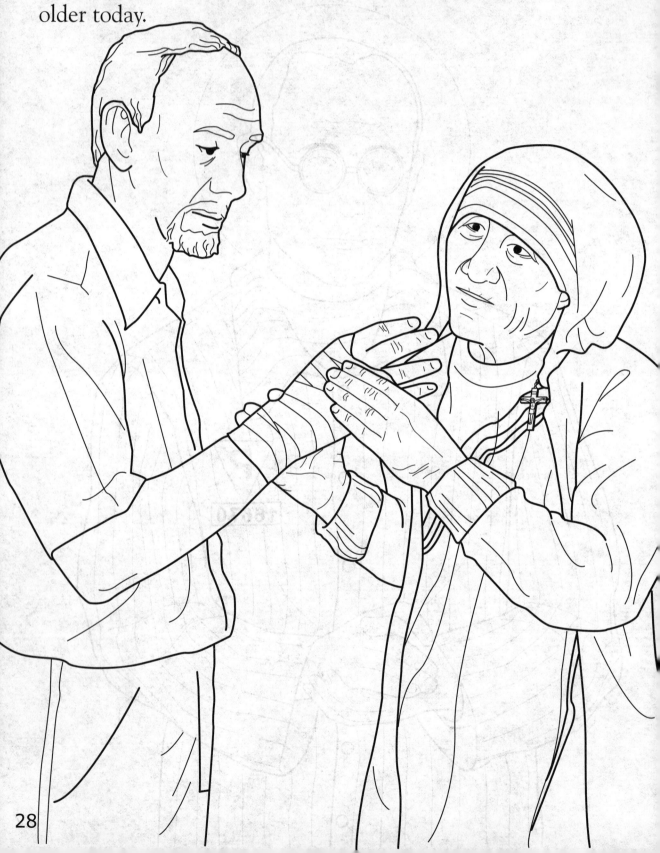

At Fatima in the country of Portugal, Our Blessed Mother appeared in 1917 to three children. They were Blessed Jacinta and Francisco Marto, and Lucia Santos. Mary asked the children to pray the Rosary for world peace. Where is your Rosary?

Saint Gianna Beretta Molla was a doctor, wife, and mother of four. Doctors wanted to abort her fourth child because a tumor was also growing in her womb, but Gianna would not let them. Thank your mother for giving birth to you.

Blessed Pope John Paul II was shot twice by a man in Saint Peter's Square in 1981. He forgave the man who shot him. When you are hurt, be forgiving to those who hurt you.

Every person—little or big—has an angel sent from God to watch over them. Thank God for your Guardian Angel, and for all the Saints who love you and pray for you!